For All the World

HELEN EARLE SIMCOX

Augsburg
MINNEAPOLIS

This book is dedicated to

Cean, Vicky, Marget, and Jonathan.

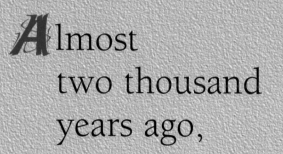

Almost
two thousand
years ago,

Jesus was born
in Bethlehem of Judea
in the land of Palestine.

And Mary, his mother,
wrapped him
in swaddling clothes
and laid him in a manger.

God chose Mary,
   a young Jewish woman,
   to be the one through whom
   all nations would be blessed.

God might have chosen someone
from a different land and
from a different time in history.

Jesus might have been born
in Sappora, Japan,

or on the Alaskan tundra,

or in Lithuania,

or in a village in Africa.

Mary and her child
might have looked
like this—

or this —

or this—

or this—

because God loves
all the peoples of the world
and children everywhere,

like True Son,

Ming Da,

Uri,

and Jill.

But in that long ago time
God chose Mary
and the little town
of Bethlehem
in the Judean hills.

And there, in Bethlehem,
God gave us Jesus—

a gift of love
for all the world.